Santa's Workshop

Vickie Clontz of Annie's Keepsakes

LEISURE ARTS, INC. • Maumelle, Arkansas

Table of Contents

About the Author

Vickie Clontz is an award-winning designer, teacher, author and fiber artist specializing in wool and all things related. Her pattern company, Annie's Keepsakes, has over 130 original designs for sewing, quilting, home decor, and wearables, and is celebrating 32 years of business in 2022! Vickie loves sharing her talent, skills and expertise with others through the workshops she teaches across the country and abroad. Vickie's designs have been published in numerous magazines and publications in the US and around the world, and she has written 5 books for Leisure Arts on quick 'n easy sewing projects. She is also excited to be hosting a "Fantasy Fabric Tour of France" in September of 2023 that will truly be the trip of a lifetime! For more details, please visit her at annieskeepsakes.com

Santa's Workshop

Finished Size: approximately 7$^1/_2$" x 9$^1/_4$" (19.1 cm x 23.5 cm)

SHOPPING LIST

- ☐ 16" x 16" (40.6 cm x 40.6 cm) square of red Woolfelt®
- ☐ 14" x 14" (35.6 cm x 35.6 cm) square of white Woolfelt®
- ☐ 3" x 8" (7.6 cm x 20.3 cm) piece of aqua Woolfelt®
- ☐ 3" x 6" (7.6 cm x 15.2 cm) piece of yellow Woolfelt®
- ☐ 3" x 7" (7.6 cm x 17.8 cm) piece of green Woolfelt®
- ☐ 3" x 5" (7.6 cm x 12.7 cm) piece of orange Woolfelt®
- ☐ 20" x 20" (50.8 cm x 50.8 cm) square of lightweight fusible interfacing

You will also need:

- ☐ Embroidery floss: white, red, and green
- ☐ Embroidery needle
- ☐ Polyester fiberfill
- ☐ Air-erasable fabric marking pen.
- ☐ Aleene's® Tacky Glue (optional)

CUTTING THE PIECES

All measurements include seam allowances.

From red Woolfelt®:

- Cut 1 **base** 5" x 5$^1/_4$".
- Cut 2 **sides** 4$^3/_4$" x 5".
- Cut 1 **workshop front.**
- Cut 1 **workshop back.**
- Cut 2 **hearts.**
- Cut 1 **doorknob.**

From white Woolfelt®:

- Cut 2 **roof rectangles** 5" x 6$^1/_4$".
- Cut 2 **front/back snow.**
- Cut 2 **side snows.**
- Cut 2 **candy canes.**

From aqua Woolfelt®:

- Cut 1 **door.**

From green Woolfelt®:

- Cut 2 **leaves.**
- Cut 1 **stem** $^1/_8$" x 1".
- Cut 1 **window box.**

From assorted Woolfelt® colors:

- Cut 28 assorted **circles** 1$^1/_4$" diameter, including 1 yellow circle for front window.

From lightweight fusible interfacing:

- Cut 2 **roof rectangles** 4$^3/_4$" x 6".
- Cut 1 **base** 4$^3/_4$" x 5".
- Cut 2 **sides** 4$^1/_2$" x 4$^3/_4$".
- Cut 1 **workshop front.**
- Cut 1 **workshop back.**

INSTRUCTIONS

*(**Note:** Use 2 strands of embroidery floss for all embroidery unless otherwise indicated.)*

Workshop Front

1. With upper straight edges even, Blanket Stitch inner curvy edge of front snow to workshop front using white floss.

2. Blanket Stitch 1 heart and doorknob to door using red floss. Blanket Stitch door to workshop front using 3 strands of red floss.

3. Using long, diagonal Straight Stitches to resemble stripes, sew candy canes to each side of door using 6 strands of red floss. Use a drop of glue to hold cane in place if needed.

4. Mark the outer edge of 1 yellow circle in 6 evenly spaced points. Pin yellow circle above door. Beginning each stitch at the outer edge and ending in the center, use long Straight Stitches to sew circle in place using 3 strands of red floss. Stitch a French knot in center of circle with same floss.

Workshop Back

5. With upper straight edges even, Blanket Stitch inner curvy edge of back snow to workshop back using white floss.

6. Blanket Stitch remaining heart to window box using red floss. Blanket Stitch window box to workshop back using green floss. Use a Running Stitch to sew stem and leaves to workshop back using green floss. Sew 3 flower circles to workshop back in same manner as workshop front window with 3 strands of red floss.

Roof

7. Evenly space 12 circles on each roof rectangle. Sew circles to each roof rectangle in the same manner you sewed the previous circles.

Assembling the Workshop

*(**Note:** When assembling workshop, place pieces with back sides together.)*

8. Trim fusible interfacing for the workshop front and back $^1/_8$" smaller on all sides than corresponding Woolfelt pieces.

9. Fuse interfacing to back side of front, back, sides, and roof rectangles.

10. Blanket Stitch lower edge of 1 roof rectangle to upper edge of 1 side using white floss. Repeat for remaining roof and side.

11. Blanket Stitch upper edge of roof rectangles together using white floss.

12. Blanket Stitch workshop front to sides and roof using corresponding color floss as needed. Repeat for workshop back.

13. Stuff workshop firmly with fiberfill. Blanket Stitch base to bottom using red floss.

Doorknob
Cut 1

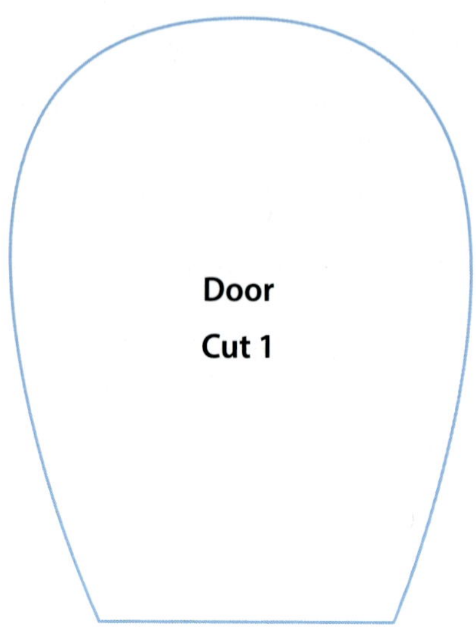

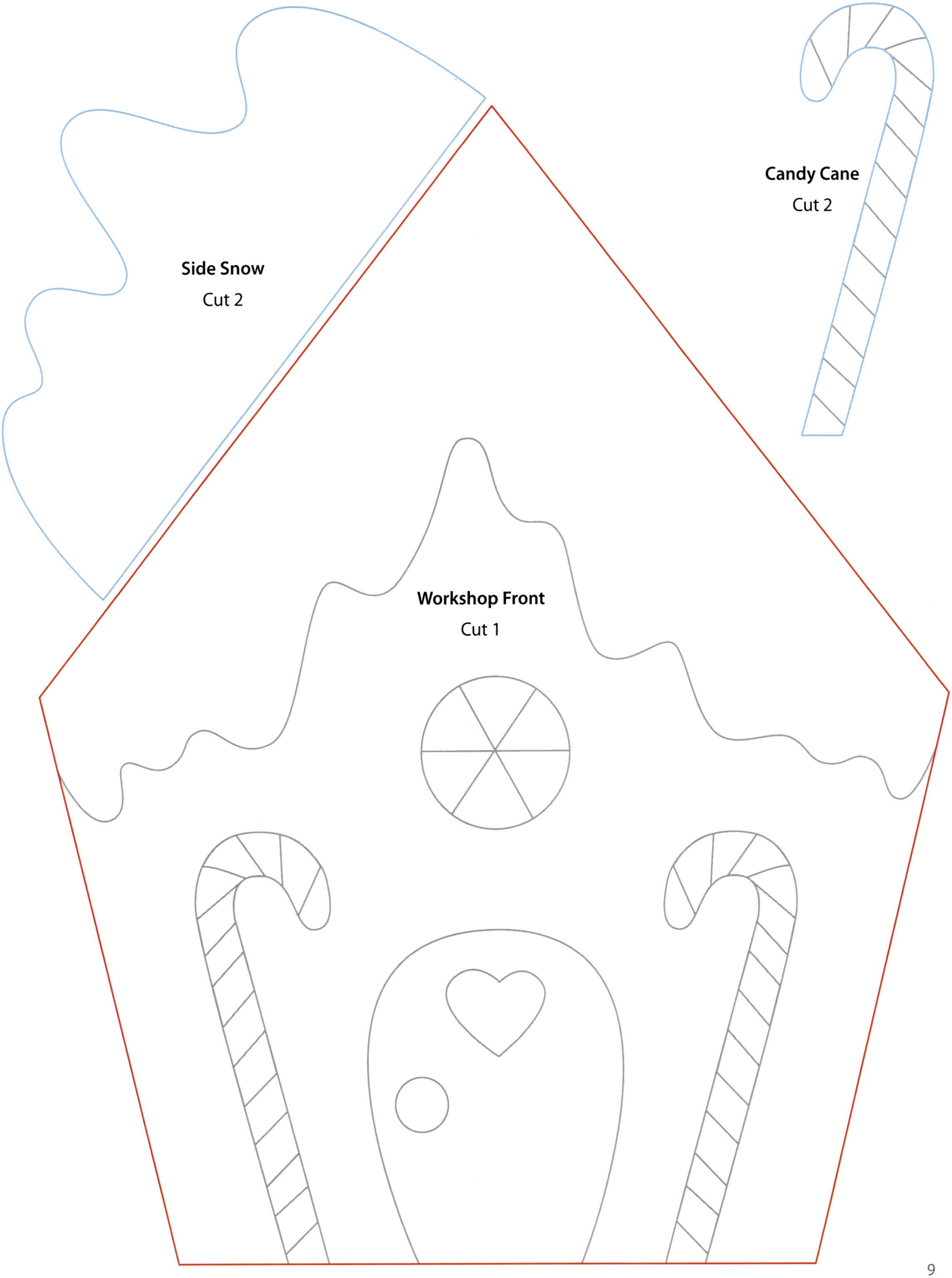
Side Snow
Cut 2
Candy Cane
Cut 2
Workshop Front
Cut 1

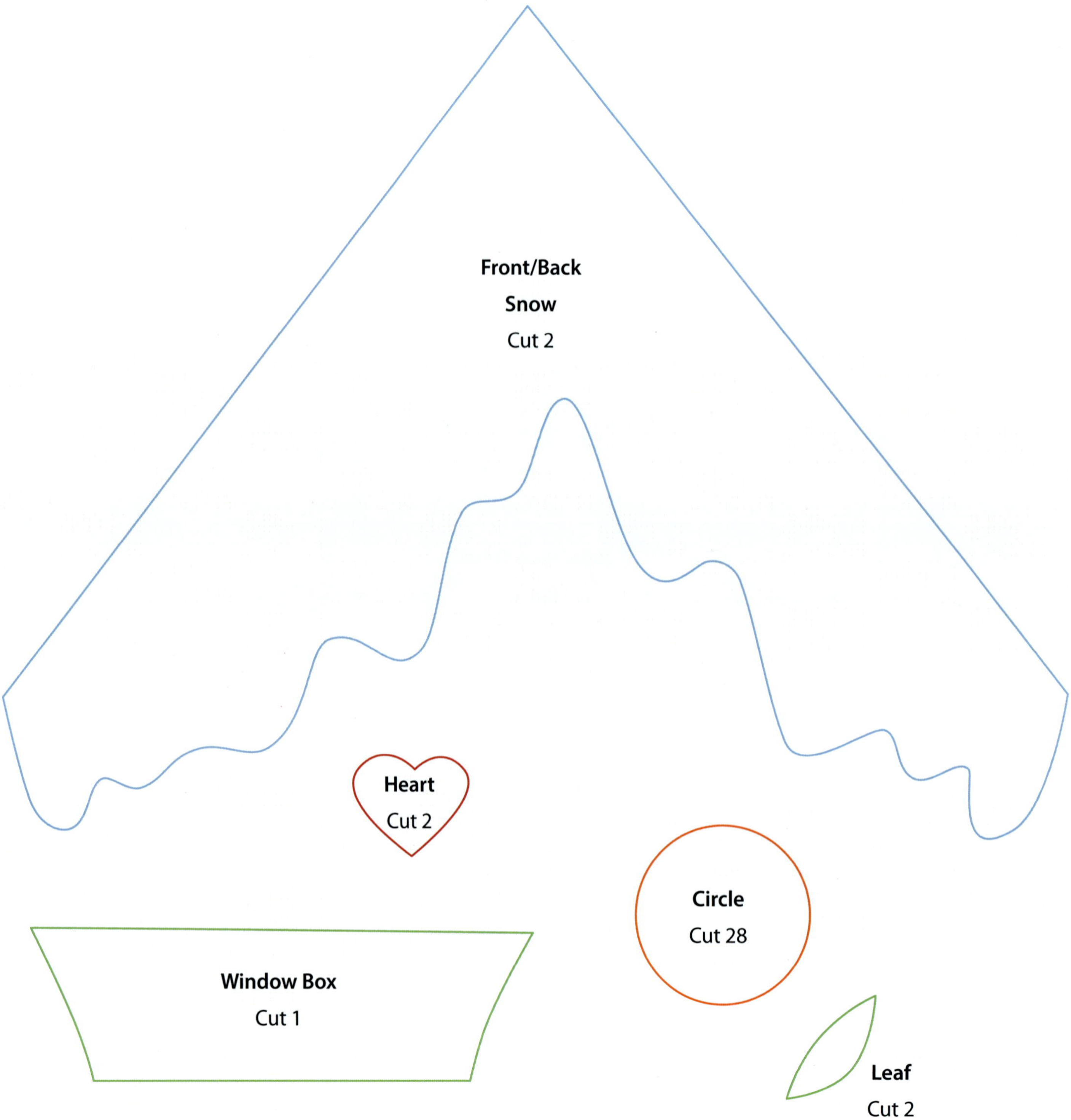
Front/Back
Snow
Cut 2
Heart
Cut 2
Circle
Cut 28
Window Box
Cut 1
Leaf
Cut 2

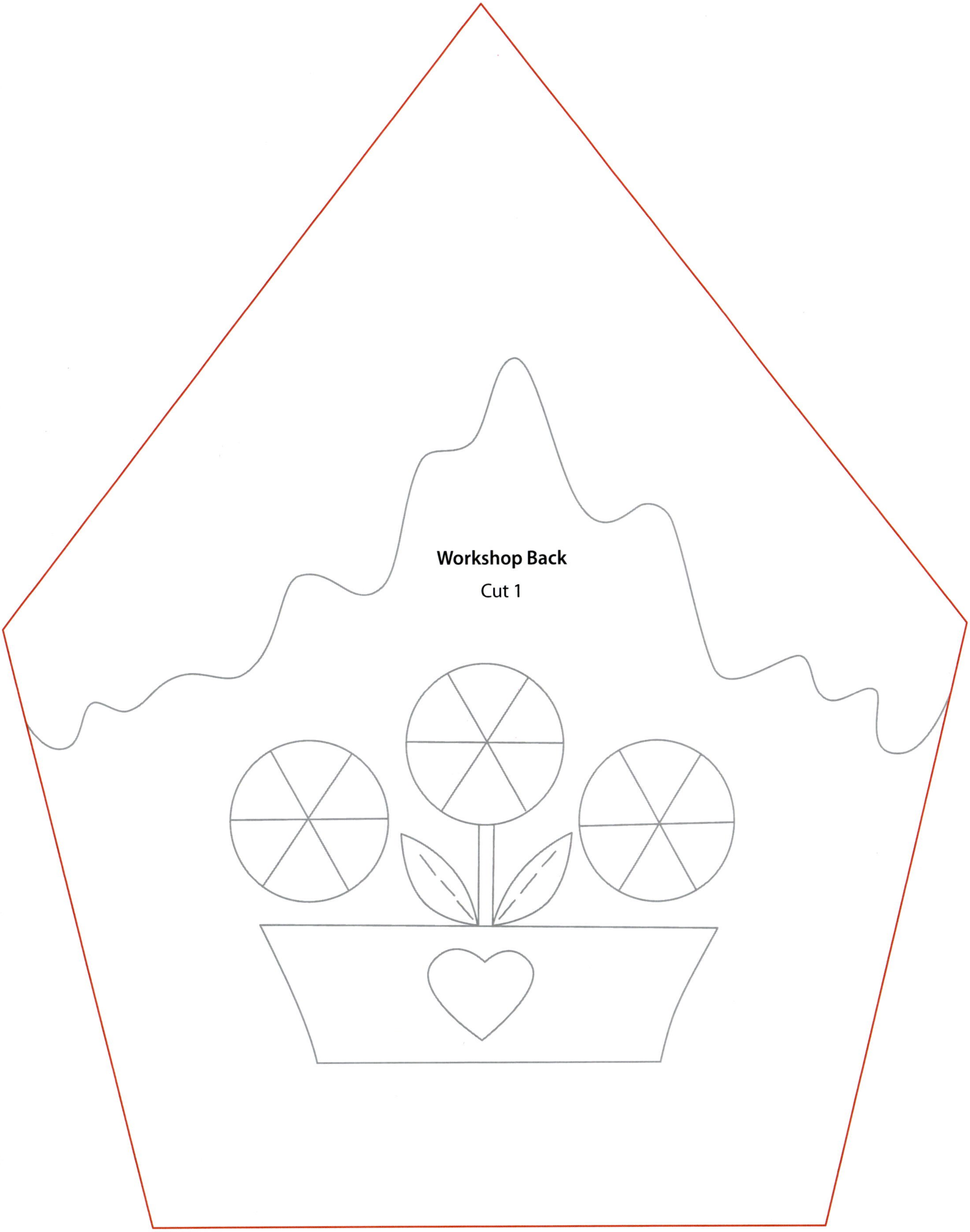
Workshop Back
Cut 1

Santa's Workshop Tree

Finished Size: approximately 3¾" x 6½" (9.5 cm x 16.5 cm)

SHOPPING LIST

- ☐ 9" x 11" (22.9 cm x 27.9 cm) piece of green Woolfelt®
- ☐ 4" x 4" (10.2 cm x 10.2 cm) square of white Woolfelt®
- ☐ Seven 1½" x 1½" (3.8 cm x 3.8 cm) squares of assorted colors of Woolfelt® (I used 4 different colors.)
- ☐ 9" x 11" (22.9 cm x 27.9 cm) piece of lightweight fusible interfacing

You will also need:

- ☐ Sewing thread: green
- ☐ Embroidery floss: white, red, and green
- ☐ Embroidery needle
- ☐ Polyester fiberfill
- ☐ Air-erasable fabric marking pen.

CUTTING THE PIECES

All measurements include seam allowances.

From green Woolfelt®:

- Cut 1 **tree**.
- Cut 1 **tree base**.

From white Woolfelt®:

- Cut 1 **snow top**.

From assorted colors of Woolfelt®:

- Cut 7 **circles**.

From lightweight fusible interfacing:

- Cut 1 **tree**.
- Cut 1 **tree base**.

INSTRUCTIONS

*(**Note:** Use 2 strands of embroidery floss for all embroidery unless otherwise indicated.)*

1. Transfer snow and circle placement to tree.

2. Stack snow top on top of tree. Blanket Stitch snow top to tree along inner curvy edge using white floss. Baste upper straight edges together.

3. Mark the outer edge of 1 circle in 6 evenly spaced points. Pin circle to tree. Beginning each stitch at the outer edge and ending in the center, use long Straight Stitches to sew circle in place using 3 strands of red floss. Stitch a French knot in center of circle with same floss. Repeat for remaining circles.

4. Trim away some of the interfacing at upper point of tree to reduce bulk for easier turning. Fuse interfacing to back of tree and tree base.

5. Matching front sides, pin long straight sides together; hand or machine stitch with green thread using a 1/4" seam allowance. Press seam allowances open. Turn tree right side out, pushing out upper point.

6. Stuff tree firmly. Blanket Stitch tree base to bottom edge of tree with edges even using green floss.

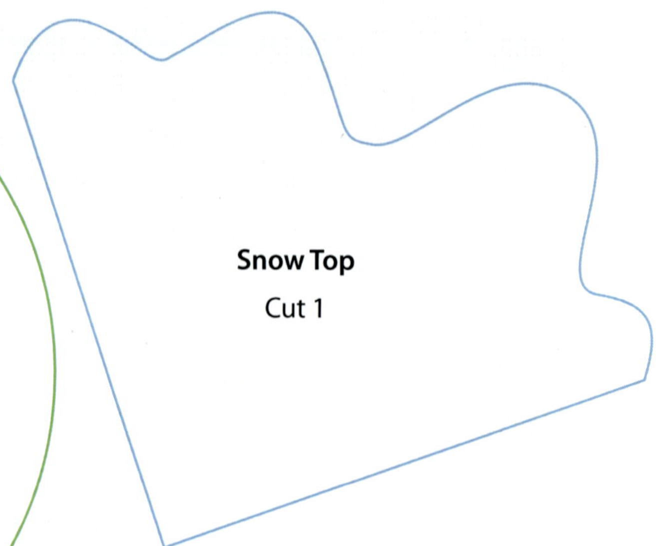

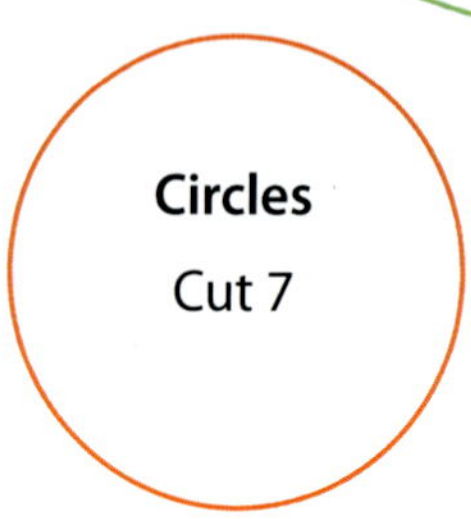

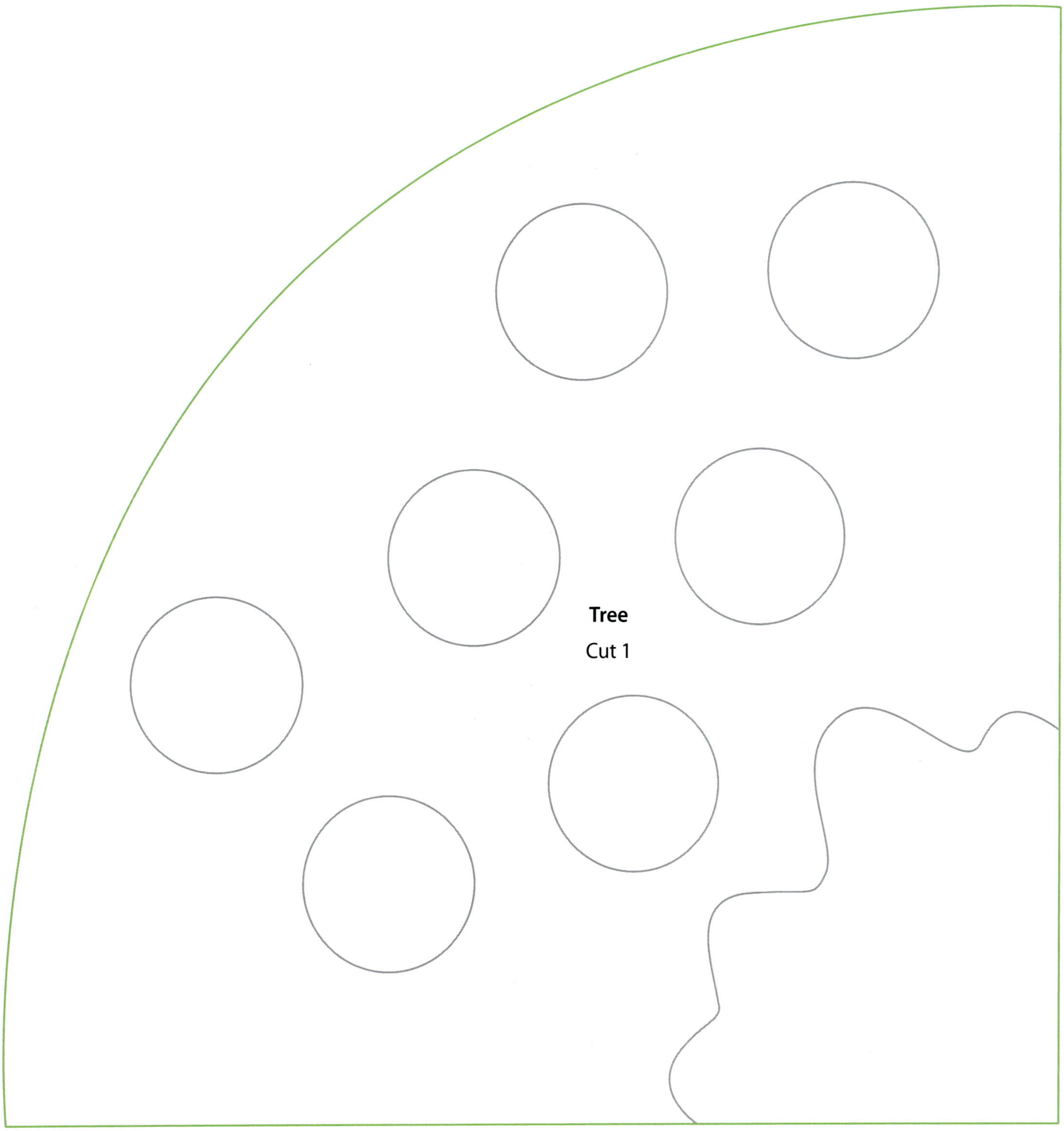
Tree
Cut 1

Santa Ornament

Finished Size: approximately 3$^1/_2$" x 5" (8.9 cm x 12.7 cm)

SHOPPING LIST

- ☐ 7" x 8" (17.8 cm x 20.3 cm) piece of red Woolfelt®
- ☐ 4" x 4" (10.2 cm x 10.2 cm) square of white Woolfelt®
- ☐ $^3/_4$" x 2" (1.9 cm x 5.1 cm) piece of black Woolfelt®
- ☐ 3" x 4" (7.6 cm x 10.2 cm) piece of flesh Woolfelt®
- ☐ $^1/_2$" x $^3/_8$" (1.3 cm x 1 cm) piece of yellow Woolfelt®
- ☐ Embroidery floss: red, black, and white
- ☐ Embroidery needle
- ☐ Sewing thread: red
- ☐ 9" (22.9 cm) length of red $^1/_8$" (3mm) ribbon or cording
- ☐ Small amount of polyester fiberfill
- ☐ Air-erasable fabric marking pen.
- ☐ Aleene's® Tacky Glue

CUTTING THE PIECES

All measurements include seam allowances.

From red Woolfelt®:

- Cut 2 **bodies**.
- Cut 2 **hats**.

From white Woolfelt®:

- Cut 1 **hat brim**.
- Cut 2 **pompoms**.
- Cut 1 **beard**.
- Cut 1 **moustache**.
- Cut 1 **coat trim** $^1/_4$" x 4".

From black Woolfelt®:

- Cut 2 **eyes**.
- Cut 1 **belt** $^1/_4$" x 2".

From flesh Woolfelt®:

- Cut 1 **face**.

From yellow Woolfelt®:

- Cut 1 **buckle**.

INSTRUCTIONS

*(**Note:** Use 2 strands of embroidery floss for all embroidery unless otherwise indicated.)*

1. Transfer markings for eyebrows and eyes to face.

2. Backstitch eyebrows using black floss. Blanket Stitch eyes in place using black floss.

3. Pin 1 hat and face on 1 body so that edges meet; pin beard to lower face so that edges overlap slightly. Whipstitch lower hat edge and upper edge of face together using 1 strand of white floss. Blanket Stitch upper edge of beard to face using white floss. Blanket Stitch moustache over beard using white floss. Blanket Stitch hat band over lower hat and upper face using white floss.

4. Blanket Stitch coat trim to arms and lower body using white floss, trimming lengths even with outer edges. Blanket Stitch belt above white trim just under arms using black floss.

5. With back sides facing, place Santa front on Santa back. Pin remaining hat to top of body back with outer hat edges even. Stitching through back only (not front), Blanket Stitch lower edge of hat back to back using red floss. Blanket Stitch lower body, arms, and legs together using red floss; stuff lightly. Blanket Stitch around beard and hat band using white floss; stuff lightly.

6. To make hanging loop, fold ribbon or cording in half; knot ends. Hand or machine sew knot 1/4" below upper edge of head on body back using red thread.

7. Blanket Stitch hat front to back using red floss. Blanket Stitch pompoms to hat tip with tip sandwiched in between using white floss.

8. Glue yellow belt buckle to black belt.

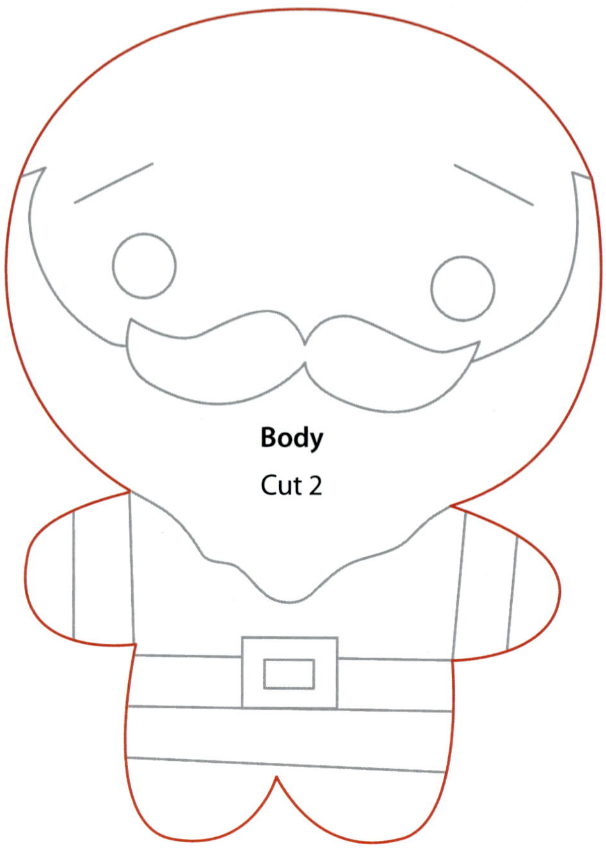

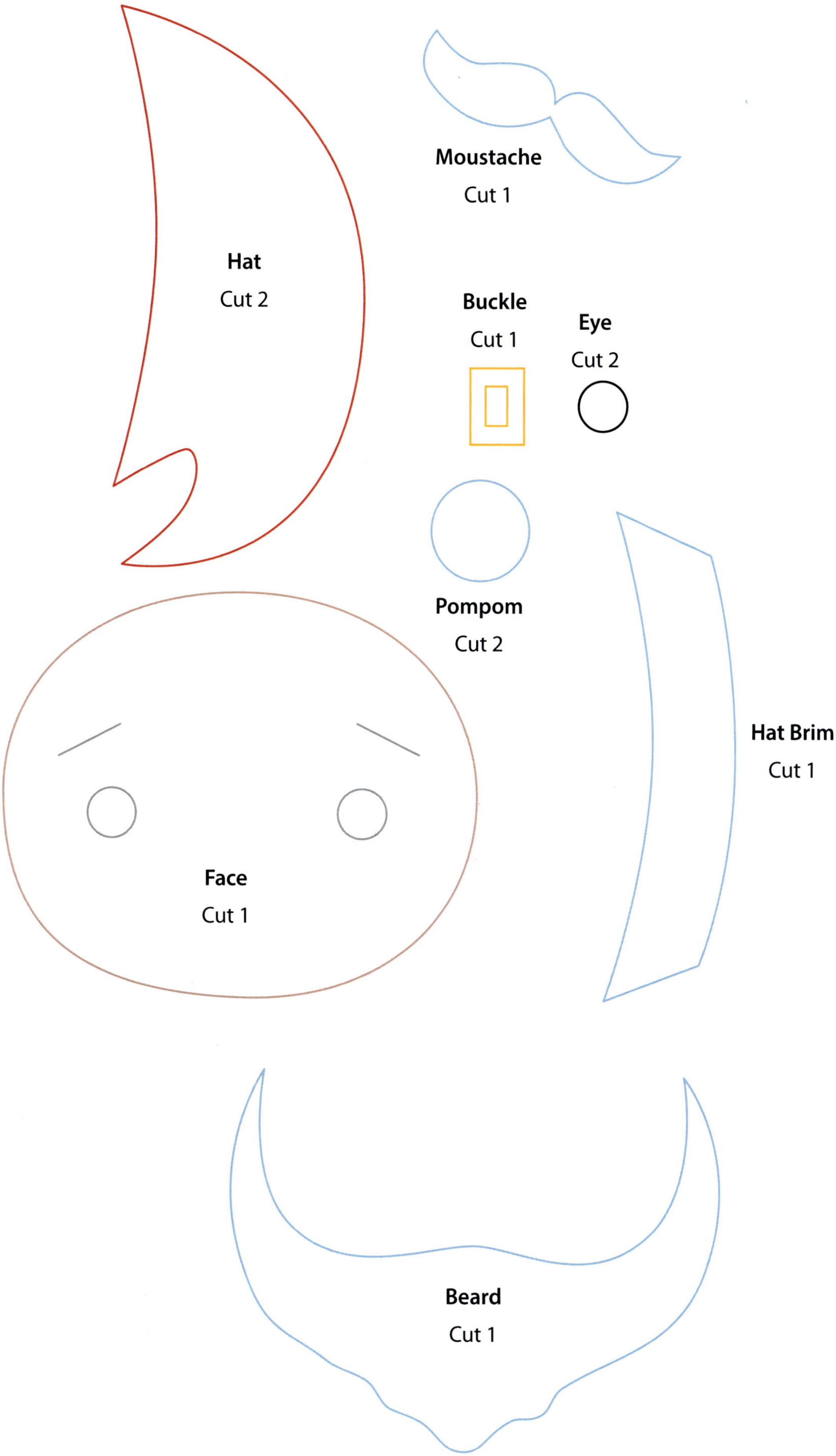
Moustache
Cut 1
Hat
Cut 2
Buckle
Cut 1
Eye
Cut 2
Pompom
Cut 2
Hat Brim
Cut 1
Face
Cut 1
Beard
Cut 1

Mrs. Claus Ornament

Finished Size: approximately 3$^1/_2$" x 5" (8.9 cm x 12.7 cm)

SHOPPING LIST

- ☐ 6" x 8" (15.2 cm x 20.3 cm) piece of red Woolfelt®
- ☐ 6" x 7" (15.2 cm x 17.8 cm) piece of white Woolfelt®
- ☐ $^3/_4$" x 1$^1/_4$" (1.9 cm x 3.2 cm) piece of black Woolfelt®
- ☐ 4" x 4" (10.2 cm x 10.2 cm) square of flesh Woolfelt®
- ☐ 1" x 1" (2.5 cm x 2.5 cm) square of green Woolfelt®
- ☐ Embroidery floss: red, black, white, green, and flesh
- ☐ Embroidery needle
- ☐ Sewing thread: white
- ☐ 9" (22.9 cm) length of white $^1/_8$" (3mm) ribbon or cording
- ☐ Rotary cutter with scallop-and-peak decorative-edge blade
- ☐ Air-erasable fabric marking pen.
- ☐ Small amount of polyester fiberfill

CUTTING THE PIECES

All measurements include seam allowances.

From red Woolfelt®:

- Cut 2 **bodies.**
- Cut 1 **holly berry.**

From white Woolfelt®:

- Cut 1 **apron.**
- Cut 1 **hair front.**
- Cut 1 **hair back.**
- Cut 1 **strip** $^1/_4$" x 7" with 1 long edge cut with scallop-and-peak decorative-edge blade

From black Woolfelt®:

- Cut 2 **eyes.**

From flesh Woolfelt®:

- Cut 1 **face.**

From green Woolfelt®:

- Cut 2 **holly leaves.**

INSTRUCTIONS

*(**Note:** Use 2 strands of embroidery floss for all embroidery unless otherwise indicated.)*

1. Transfer markings for eyebrows, eyelashes, mouth, and eyes to face.

2. Backstitch eyebrows using black floss. Blanket Stitch eyes in place using black floss. Backstitch eyelashes and mouth using the same floss. Pin face to body front; pin hair front over face. Blanket Stitch inner edge of hair front to face using white floss.

3. Blanket Stitch upper edge of apron to body front below arms using white floss. Use a Running Stitch to attach scalloped strip over lower edge of apron using white floss, trimming edges to match apron. Attach scalloped strip at neck under face in the same manner. Attach scalloped strip in the same manner for 2 apron straps. Use a Running Stitch to attach holly leaves to apron using green floss. Blanket Stitch holly berry to apron using red floss.

4. With back sides facing, Blanket Stitch body front to body back using red floss; stuff lightly.

5. To make hanging loop, fold ribbon or cording in half; knot ends. Hand or machine sew knot $^1/_4$" below upper edge of head on body back using white thread.

6. Pin hair back to body back. Pin lower portion of head front to body front. Blanket Stitch lower face to head using flesh floss. Stuff head lightly. Blanket Stitch outer edge of hair together using white floss. Backstitch around base of hair bun using 6 strands of red floss.

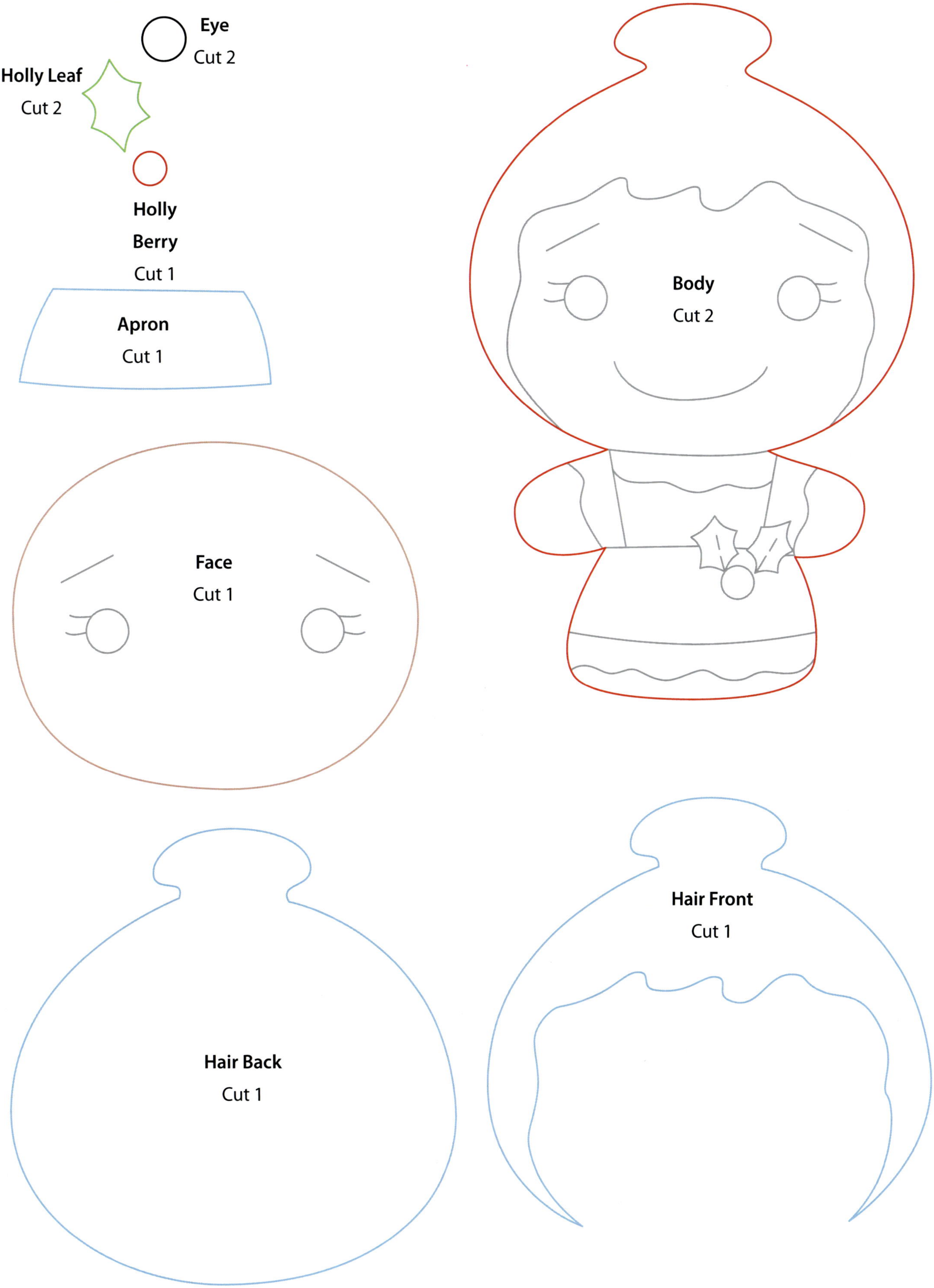
Eye
Cut 2
Holly Leaf
Cut 2
Holly
Berry
Cut 1
Apron
Cut 1
Body
Cut 2
Face
Cut 1
Hair Back
Cut 1
Hair Front
Cut 1

Elf Ornament

Finished Size: approximately 4$^{1}/_{2}$" x 5" (11.4 cm x 12.7 cm)

SHOPPING LIST

- ☐ 6" x 8" (15.2 cm x 20.3 cm) piece of red Woolfelt®
- ☐ 5" x 6" (12.7 cm x 15.2 cm) piece of green Woolfelt®
- ☐ 2" x 5" (5.1 cm x 12.7 cm) piece of black Woolfelt®
- ☐ 3" x 5" (7.6 cm x 12.7 cm) piece of flesh Woolfelt®
- ☐ 1$^{1}/_{2}$" x 1$^{1}/_{2}$" (3.8 cm x 3.8 cm) piece of yellow Woolfelt®
- ☐ $^{1}/_{4}$" x 2$^{1}/_{2}$" (0.6 cm x 6.4 cm) piece of white Woolfelt® using the scallop-and-peak decorative-edge blade to cut 1 long edge
- ☐ 4" x 5" (10.2 cm x 12.7 cm) piece of brown Woolfelt®
- ☐ Embroidery floss: red, black, white, green, brown, yellow, and flesh
- ☐ Embroidery needle
- ☐ Sewing thread: green
- ☐ 9" (22.9 cm) length of white $^{1}/_{8}$" (3mm) ribbon or cording
- ☐ Rotary cutter with scallop-and-peak decorative-edge blade
- ☐ Air-erasable fabric marking pen.
- ☐ Small amount of polyester fiberfill
- ☐ Aleene's® Tacky Glue

CUTTING THE PIECES

All measurements include seam allowances.

From red Woolfelt®:

- Cut 2 **bodies.**
- Cut 2 **hat brims.**

From green Woolfelt®:

- Cut 2 **hats.**
- Cut 2 **tunics.**

From black Woolfelt®:

- Cut 2 **eyes.**
- Cut 1 **belt** $^{1}/_{4}$" x 4".

From flesh Woolfelt®:

- Cut 1 **face.**

From yellow Woolfelt®:

- Cut 1 **buckle.**
- Cut 2 **pompoms.**

From brown Woolfelt®:

- Cut 1 **hair front.**
- Cut 1 **hair back.**

INSTRUCTIONS

*(**Note:** Use 2 strands of embroidery floss for all embroidery unless otherwise indicated.)*

1. Transfer markings for eyebrows, mouth and eyes to face.

2. Backstitch eyebrows and mouth using black floss. Blanket Stitch eyes in place using black floss.

3. Blanket Stitch hair front to face along inner edge using brown floss. Blanket Stitch hair back to body back using brown floss.

4. Blanket Stitch 1 tunic to 1 body (front) over arms and across lower edge using green floss. Repeat to attach remaining tunic to remaining body (back). Blanket Stitch upper back neck edge using the same floss. Trimming sides to fit, Blanket Stitch belt below arms on front and back using black floss.

5. Blanket Stitch face to body front at neck using flesh floss.

6. For collar, use a Running Stitch to attach white strip to front neck edge using white floss, trimming ends to fit.

7. Aligning lower edges, stack 1 hat band on hat front and hat back. Blanket Stitch upper jagged edge of hat bands to lower edge of hat front and back using red floss. Blanket Stitch hat to face on front and hair on back and Blanket Stitch lower edge of hat band in place using red floss.

8. With back sides facing, stack body front and body back. Blanket Stitch body front to body back around arms, tunic, and legs using red floss; stuff lightly. Blanket Stitch lower edge of face front to lower edge of head back using flesh floss; stuff lightly. Blanket Stitch hair back at ears using brown floss.

9. To make hanging loop, fold ribbon or cording in half; knot ends. Hand or machine sew knot 1/4" below upper edge of head on body back using green thread.

10. Blanket Stitch hat front and back using green floss, stuffing lightly before you close. Blanket Stitch pompoms to hat tip with tip sandwiched in between using yellow floss.

11. Glue buckle to belt.

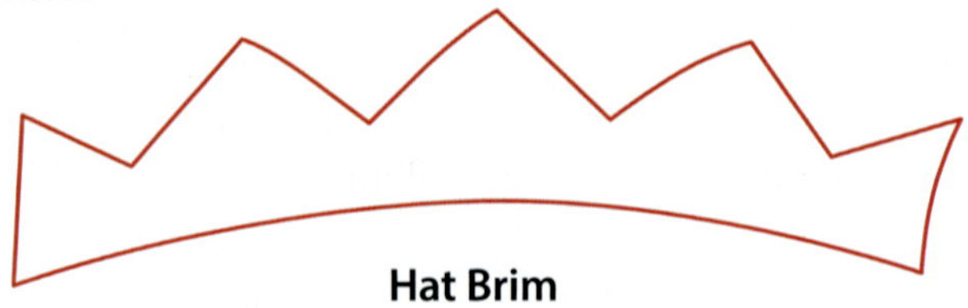

Hat Brim
Cut 2

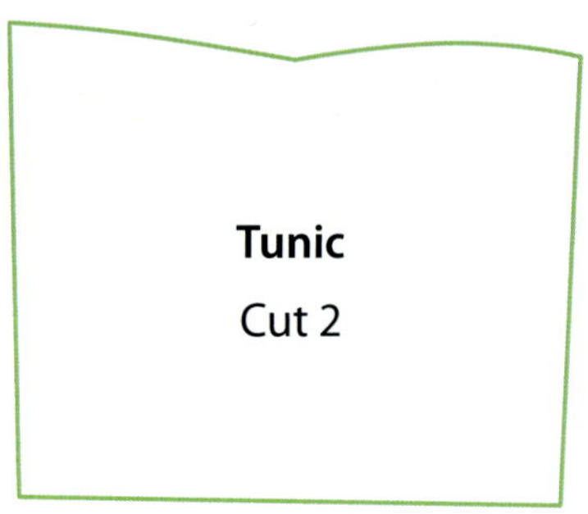

Body
Cut 2
Eye
Cut 2
Hat
Cut 2
Face
Cut 1
Hair Back
Cut 1
Hair Front
Cut 1
Pompom
Cut 2
Buckle
Cut 1

Snowman Ornament

Finished Size: approximately $4^1/_2$" x $5^1/_2$" (11.4 cm x 14 cm)

SHOPPING LIST

- ☐ 6" x 8" (15.2 cm x 20.3 cm) piece of white Woolfelt®
- ☐ 6" x 6" (15.2 cm x 15.2 cm) square of aqua Woolfelt®
- ☐ $^1/_2$" x 1" (1.3 cm x 2.5 cm) piece of orange Woolfelt®
- ☐ $^1/_2$" x 1" (1.3 cm x 2.5 cm) piece of black Woolfelt®
- ☐ $^3/_8$" x 12" (1 cm x 30.5 cm) strip of red Woolfelt®
- ☐ $^3/_4$" x $1^1/_2$" (1.9 cm x 3.8 cm) piece of red Woolfelt®
- ☐ 9" (22.9 cm) length of $^1/_8$" (3.2 mm) aqua ribbon or cording
- ☐ Embroidery floss: white, black, red, orange, and aqua
- ☐ Embroidery needle
- ☐ Sewing thread: aqua
- ☐ Air-erasable fabric marking pen.
- ☐ Small amount of polyester fiberfill

CUTTING THE PIECES

All measurements include seam allowances.

From white Woolfelt®:

- Cut 2 **bodies.**

From aqua Woolfelt®:

- Cut 2 **hats.**
- Cut 1 **hat brim.**

From orange Woolfelt®:

- Cut 1 **nose.**

From black Woolfelt®:

- Cut 2 **eyes.**

From red Woolfelt®:

- Cut 2 **pompoms.**

INSTRUCTIONS

*(**Note:** Use 2 strands of embroidery floss for all embroidery unless otherwise indicated.)*

1. Transfer markings for eyebrows, mouth, and eyes to 1 body.

2. Backstitch eyebrows using black floss. Blanket Stitch eyes to face using black floss. Make French Knots for mouth using 6 strands of black floss. Blanket Stitch nose to face using orange floss.

3. With back sides facing, stack body front and body back. Beginning at bottom of hat placement line and stopping at lower hat placement line on the other side, Blanket Stitch outer edges together using white floss; stuff lightly. Continue stitching across top of head to close.

4. Pin hat brim to bottom of 1 hat. Blanket Stitch upper edge of brim to 1 hat (front) using aqua floss. Stack the 2 hats on snowman with head in between. Blanket Stitch lower edge of front brim to head front using aqua floss; continue around to lower edge of hat on back of head.

5. To make hanging loop, fold ribbon or cording in half; knot ends. Hand or machine sew knot $^{1}/_{4}$" below upper edge of hat back using aqua thread.

6. Blanket Stitch outer edges of hat together using aqua floss. Blanket Stitch the 2 pompoms to tip of hat with tip sandwiched in between using red floss.

7. Tie scarf around neck and knot to one side. Trim about 1" from ends so that they're even; cut 4 fringes on each end $^{3}/_{8}$" long.

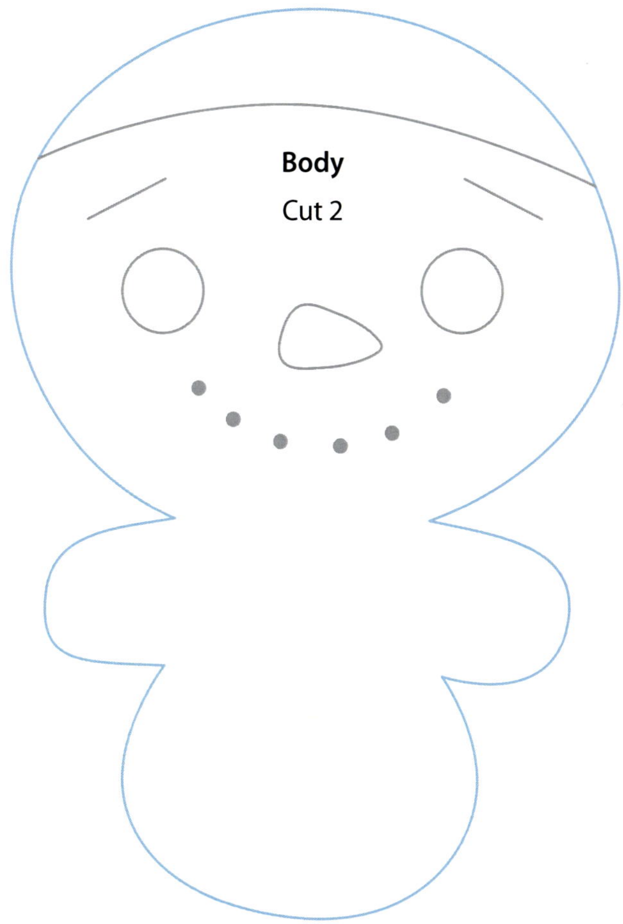
Body
Cut 2

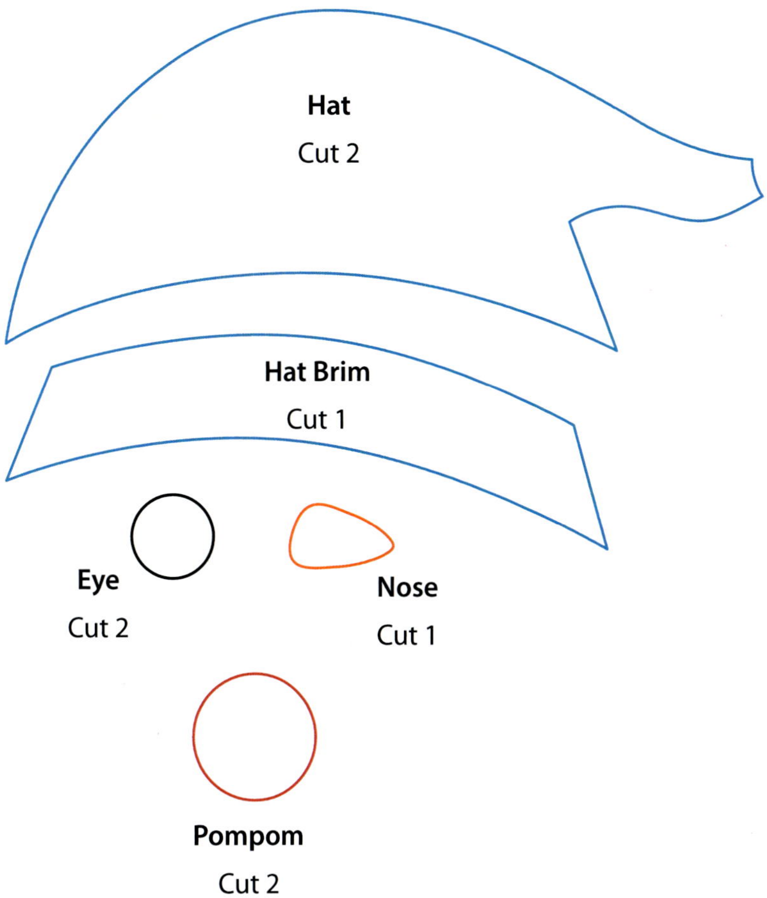
Hat
Cut 2
Hat Brim
Cut 1
Eye
Cut 2
Nose
Cut 1
Pompom
Cut 2

Santa's Workshop Ornament

Finished Size: approximately 4$^{1}/_{4}$" x 5$^{1}/_{4}$" (10.8 cm x 13.3 cm)

SHOPPING LIST

- ☐ 6" x 10" (15.2 cm x 25.4 cm) piece of aqua Woolfelt®
- ☐ 5" x 5" (12.7 cm x 12.7 cm) square of white Woolfelt®
- ☐ 2" x 2" (5.1 cm x 5.1 cm) square of red Woolfelt®
- ☐ 1" x 1" (2.5 cm x 2.5 cm) square of yellow Woolfelt®
- ☐ $^{1}/_{2}$" x $^{1}/_{2}$" (1.3 cm x 1.3 cm) square of black Woolfelt®
- ☐ 9" (22.9 cm) length of $^{1}/_{8}$" (3.2 mm) white ribbon or cording
- ☐ Embroidery floss: white, red, and black
- ☐ Embroidery needle
- ☐ Sewing thread: aqua
- ☐ Small amount of polyester fiberfill
- ☐ Rotary cutter with scallop-and-peak decorative-edge blade or pinking shears
- ☐ Air-erasable fabric marking pen.
- ☐ Aleene's® Tacky Glue (optional)

CUTTING THE PIECES

All measurements include seam allowances.

From aqua Woolfelt®:

- Cut 2 **workshops.**

From white Woolfelt®:

- Cut 1 **roof.**
- Cut 2 **candy canes.**

From red Woolfelt®:

- Cut 1 **door**

.

From yellow Woolfelt®:

- Cut 1 **window.**

From black Woolfelt®:

- Cut 1 **doorknob.**

INSTRUCTIONS

*(**Note:** Use 2 strands of embroidery floss for all embroidery unless otherwise indicated.)*

1. Blanket Stitch inner curvy edge of roof to upper workshop front using white floss.

2. Blanket Stitch door knob to door using black floss. Blanket Stitch door to lower front of workshop front using red floss.

3. Using long, diagonal Straight Stitches to resemble stripes, sew candy canes to each side of door using 6 strands of red floss. Use a drop of glue to hold cane in place if needed.

4. Mark the outer edge of 1 window in 6 evenly spaced points. Pin window above door. Beginning each stitch at the outer edge and ending in the center, use long Straight Stitches to sew window in place using 3 strands of red floss. Stitch a French knot in center of window using same floss.

5. To make hanging loop, fold ribbon or cording in half; knot ends. Hand or machine sew knot $^1/_4$" below upper edge of workshop back using aqua thread.

6. With back sides facing, place workshop front on workshop back. Beginning at one lower side, Blanket Stitch front to back at sides and upper roof using white floss; stuff lightly through lower edge. Blanket Stitch lower edges together using white floss.

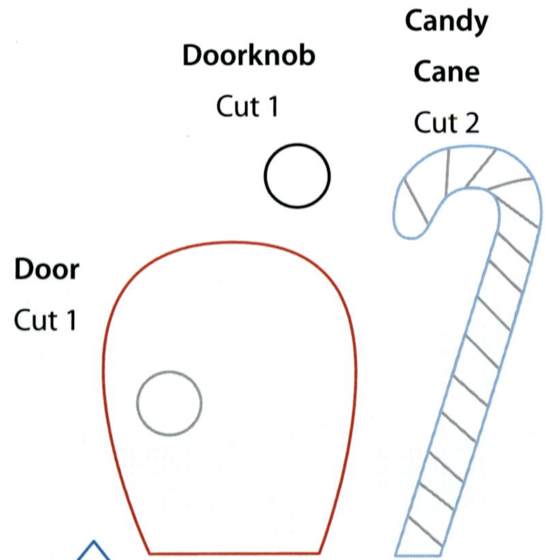

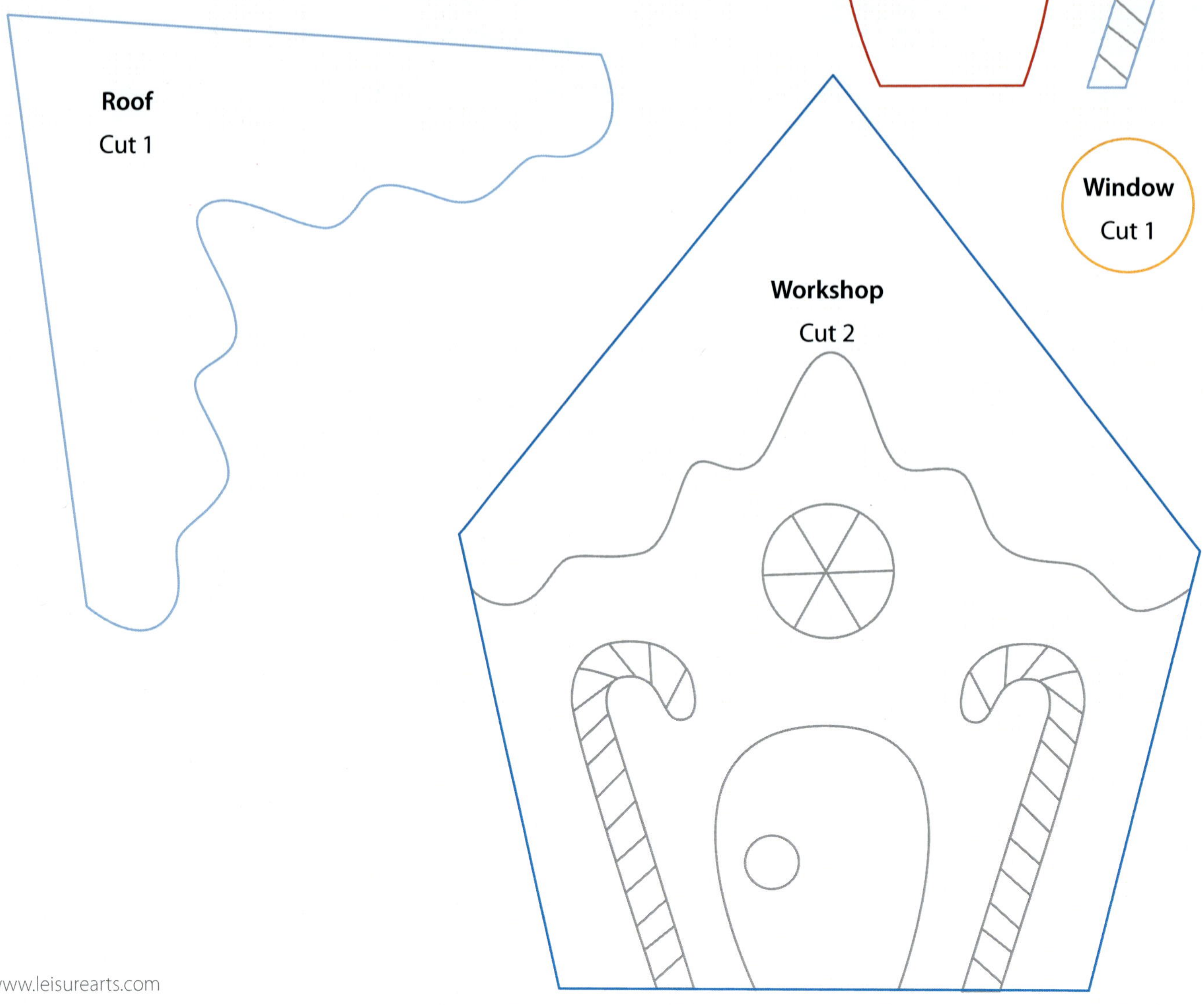

GENERAL INSTRUCTIONS

WOOL FELT

Wool felt is composed of fibers that have been compressed under heat and steam to form a textile that can be sewn with little to no raveling. Wool felt can easily be confused with felted wool. Felted wool is woven wool fabric that has been washed in hot soapy water, rinsed in cold water, and dried in a dryer to felt or shrink to minimize fraying/raveling when cut.

I use Woolfelt®, manufactured by National Nonwovens. Woolfelt is composed of wool and rayon fibers. It has a lovely hand, is of superior quality, and comes in a wide variety of colors. I've worked with it for years!

CUTTING PIECES

Trace the pattern onto paper. Be sure to trace any interior detail lines. Make 1 paper pattern for each piece needed. Cut around the pattern on the traced line. Pin the pattern on the corresponding Woolfelt® piece. Use sharp scissors to cut out the fabric shapes along the pattern edge.

TRANSFERRING STITCHING LINES FOR MOUTHS, EYEBROWS, ETC

Place the pattern onto a small piece of corrugated cardboard and use a thick needle to poke small holes about 1/4" apart along the line you wish to transfer. Then place the pattern onto the Woolfelt piece right sides up and use transfer pen to make small dots at holes. Remove pattern and stitch along markings.

CARING FOR YOUR PROJECTS

Since these projects are used for decorative purposes, you can just clean up by wiping off occasionally with a damp cloth.

STITCH DIAGRAMS

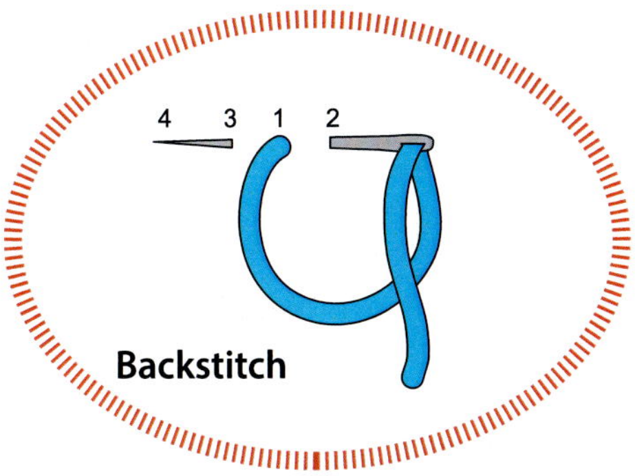

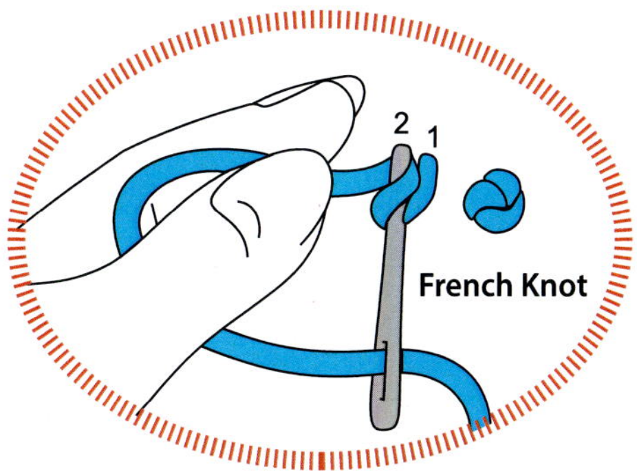

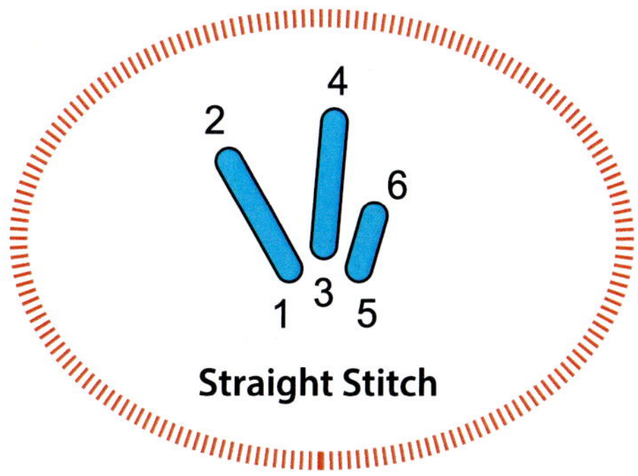

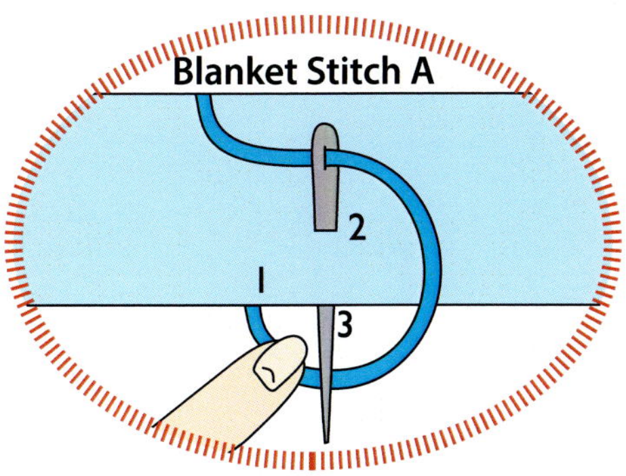

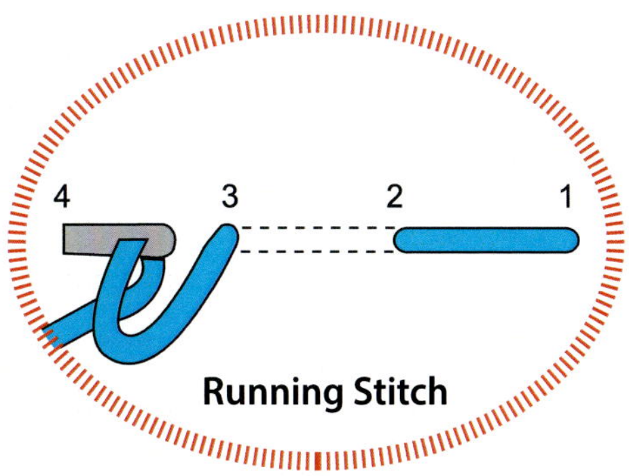

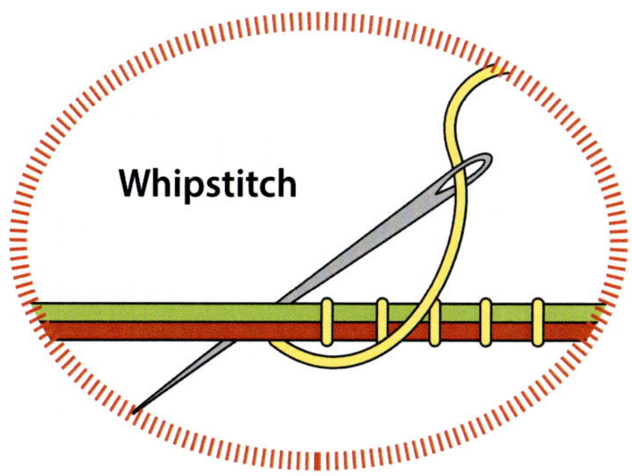

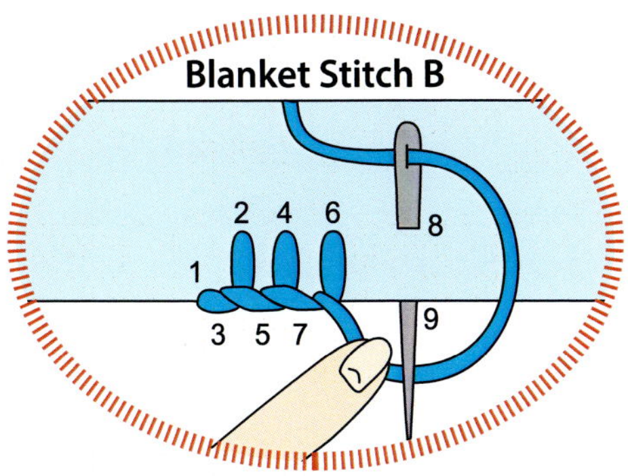

We have made every effort to ensure that these instructions are accurate and complete. We cannot, however, be responsible for human error, typographical mistakes, or variations in individual work.

Production Team: Publishing Manager – Megan Copeland; Technical Editor – Lisa Lancaster; Senior Graphic Artist – Mark Hawkins; Photographer – Rob Karman

Made in U.S.A.